A Baby's First Word Book of Wild Animals

By Judy Duppa

A Baby's First Word Book of Wild Animals

iUniverse books may be ordered through booksellers or by contacting:

iUniverse
1663 Liberty Drive
Bloomington, IN 47403
www.iuniverse.com
1-800-Authors (1-800-288-4677)

Because of the dynamic nature of the Internet, any web addresses or links contained in this book may have changed since publication and may no longer be valid. The views expressed in this work are solely those of the author and do not necessarily reflect the views of the publisher, and the publisher hereby disclaims any responsibility for them.

Any people depicted in stock imagery provided by Thinkstock are models, and such images are being used for illustrative purposes only. Certain stock imagery © Thinkstock.

ISBN: 978-1-5320-0748-4 (sc)
ISBN: 978-1-5320-0749-1 (e)

Library of Congress Control Number: 2016915509

Print information available on the last page.

iUniverse rev. date: 09/21/2016

turtle

fish

bear

8

hippopotamus

vulture

yak

dolphin

insect

17

18

kangaroo

rhinoceros

octopus

23

lion

26

camel

28

elephant

monkey

31

panda

wolf

www.ingramcontent.com/pod-product-compliance
Lightning Source LLC
Chambersburg PA
CBHW041131280526
45792CB00013B/2386